My Affection for Borth-y-Gest

Through Photographs and Postcards

Norman Spragg

authorhouse

AuthorHouse™ UK Ltd.
500 Avebury Boulevard
Central Milton Keynes, MK9 2BE
www.authorhouse.co.uk
Phone: 08001974150

First published by AuthorHouse   6/16/2011.

ISBN: 978-1-4520-1389-3 (sc)

This book is printed on acid-free paper.

Acknowledgements

Gwynedd Archives,Museums and Arts Service
Francis Frith & Co Postcards

Borth-y-Gest is a small village, at the heel of the Lleyn Peninsula, one mile west of the old sailing port of Porthmadog. This Salmon watercolour map postcard shows its position on the River Glaslyn.

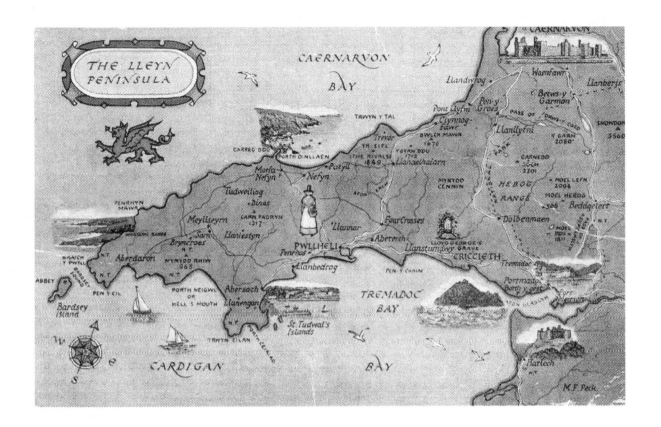

These two postcards show the village of Borth-Gest.
The first published by R. Griffiths of the local Post-Office.

The second by Salmon again.

BORTH-Y-GEST "Harbour of the Paunch"
Porth (Harbour, cove), y (the), cest (paunch, hollow)

It is thought that Borth-y-Gest got its name from the hill, which dominates, to the North of the harbour. This was called Gest in 1306 and Moel-y-Gest today.(Moel meaning bare hill). The shape of the hill resembles a paunch or big belly and this gave the name of Gest to the settlement in medieval times. Some people think that the belly could figuratively mean a bog or hollow, that swallows everything and Moel -y-Gest overlooks a vast hollow or cest near Tremadoc. The harbour was known as the Gest Harbour in 1748 but as Porthmadog grew in importance, in the Mid- 19th century, it became known as Borth-y-Gest.

In this Frith postcard you can see the flat fields around Tremadog, at the foot of Moel-y-Gest. This could have been the site of the gest or bog. In the top left of the postcard you can see the Cob at Porthmadog. This was built by William Maddocks in 1811 and it formed a dam stopping the sea coming in and flooding the fields and helping to drain the bog.

Moel-y-Gest is depicted on this Salmon postcard.

These two Valentine postcards again show Moel-y-Gest, which stands behind Borth-y-Gest and lends its name to the resort.

From this postcard in the Frith series taken from the summit of Moel-y-Gest, you can see how Borth-y-Gest lies at the foot of the hill.

Borth-y-Gest is the place where I spent the first six years of my life. It's the place which has, ever since, attracted myself and my family back for summer holidays. Indeed my brother has now bought a holiday flat in nearby Porthmadog.

I lived in Borth-y-Gest with my mother and Nain and Taid (grandmother and grandfather).

My mother and father, seen on the front left of this Carfograph by W.Harwood of Criccieth, had married at the local Bethel Church.

BETHEL

Eglwys yr Annibynwyr

Borth-y-gest

Dathlu Canmlwyddiant

1867 — 1967

DYDD MERCHER, HYDREF 11, 1967

" Mae Eglwys Dduw fel dinas wych,
Yn deg i edrych arni."

My mother, at the time, had just found new employment.

She had started work with a firm of solicitors in Porthmadog. Up to June of 1941 she was employed as a secretary at Manod Slate Quarries at Blaenau Ffestiniog. During the war these quarries were chosen by Winston Churchill as a safe haven for the country's national treasures.

MANOD CAVERNS, Blaenau Ffestiniog.

"Bury them in the bowels of the earth, but not a picture shall leave this island"
Winston S. Churchill — 1940.

Due to the quarries being taken over by the Ministry of Works and Buildings, my mother moved to new employment, taking up a post with the firm of solicitors know as Messrs. William George and Sons of Porthmadog, The head of this firm was the brother of David Lloyd George, the eminent Prime Minister.

SLATES OFFERED SUBJECT
BEING UNSOLD

On Admiralty, War Office and
Crown Agents for Colonies Lists.

TELEPHONE & TELEGRAM!
FESTINIOG 5

MANOD SLATE QUARRIES LIMITED,

Blaenau-Festiniog, North Wales.

7th June 1941.

<u>TO ALL WHOM IT MAY CONCERN.</u>

We have pleasure in giving Miss. Myfanwy Davies Humphreys of Morven, Borthygest, a testimonial as follows:

Miss. Humphreys was appointed as Acting Secretary to our Company in October 1940, and although the work was quite new to her she very soon proved herself to be really useful, and able to be left in charge of all our Office work, including the accounts which had to be kept in connection with the Government Contract which started last October, and is just completed.

Miss. Humphreys is an excellent Shorthand-typist, and good at Book-keeping, and Office work in general, and is only leaving us because our Slate Quarries have been taken over by the Ministry of Works and Buildings, and to take up a post near her home, with the firm of Solicitors known as Messrs. William George & Son of Portmadoc.

We are all very sorry to loose Miss. Humphreys and cannot speak too highly of her in every way.

for, MANOD SLATE QUARRIES LIMITED,

JSMatthews.

<u>Managing Director.</u>

Two centres had been chosen to store paintings during the 2nd World War. These were the National Library in Aberystwyth and Penryn Castle in Bangor. However, with the fall of France in the war, the government was forced to think in terms of more secure storage premises. Eventually, thanks to strong recommendation from David Lloyd George to Winston Churchill, the Manod Slate Quarries were agreed upon as the ideal wartime home for the paintings.

MANOD CAVERNS

BLAENAU FFESTINIOG

THE "HOME" OF VALUABLE ART TREASURES
FROM BUCKINGHAM PALACE AND
THE NATIONAL GALLERY
DURING THE SECOND WORLD WAR.

*OFFICIAL BROCHURE TO MARK THE OPENING
OF THE 'MYSTERY' CAVERNS TO THE PUBLIC
ON SATURDAY, SEPTEMBER 24th 1983.*

A postcard of Blaenau Ffestiniog, published by Valentine & Sons Ltd., and it was in the hills behind that Manod Slate Quarry was situated.

BLAENAU FFESTINIOG. (11)

At the time of my birth, in 1942, my father was serving in the army in Ceylon, now Sri Lanka. Here he was training soldiers prior going to fight in Burma.

My father stands second from the right on the back row of this regimental photograph.

We lived in a small terraced house on the front at Borth-y-Gest. The house was called Morven and got its name from the Morven Hills in Scotland not far from Glasgow on the River Clyde. Taid was an intrepid seaman and Glasgow was one of his ports of calls.

These two postcards show our house on the front, to the left of the gap behind the shed with the white roof. The first a real photographic postcard by Kingsway, the second an old card in the Wykeham Collection.

These two postcards again show Morven facing the beautiful bay at Borth-y-Gest. The first published by Pictorial Stationary, the second by Frith

The Harbour, Borth-y-Gest

Next door to Morven was the Igloo Café, now an established restaurant. In this postcard by Frith, Taid can be seen sitting outside on the right. The owner of the café was Mrs Tipps and I can recall that the ice cream she made was the best around. In the many summer holidays I had at Morven I was a regular visitor to the Igloo. I can remember that on the final day of my holidays, the last thing I did was to go for an ice cream and recall how overjoyed I was when Mrs Tipps said it was free.

I attended the local school Ysgol Borth-y-Gest, for three years, before my father returned from the war and moved to live in England, to his home near Liverpool,

This is the same school my mother had attended in the 1920's as this photograph shows, taken in 1928. My mother is in the middle of the row of girls standing.

Borth-y-Gest was once a thriving village and in its heyday in the 1870's and 1880's, had up to four shipyards constructing Ocean Liners Sailing Ships. These were built using local wood from Welsh oaks growing in Borth Woods. These ships travelled all over the world.

These two old postcards, the first by Frith and the second by Photochrome Ltd., show the old sailing ships in the Traeth (or bay).

The next two photographs are by kind permission of the Gwynedd Archives.

The first one is looking towards Tai Pilot (Pilot Houses), the larger houses on the left. The pilots were stationed here so that they could keep a good look out down the estuary for vessels needing their services. One of the boat yards can be seen on the right, near to the sheds, where today the parking ground is situated.

In the second photograph, this time looking from the Tai Pilot, the fishing boat Pearl can be seen. Across the Traeth, on the right behind Pearl, is the slipway at Craig-y-Don, where ships were also built.

This postcard by Frith shows the Traeth at the height of its boat building days. There were three yards on the Traeth building the beautiful Ocean Liners. Among the owners were Richard Jones and Simon Jones, who built the Ocean Monarch in 1851.

Two postcards by kind permission of Gwynedd Archives.

A closer view of the Pearl in full sail.

These three children sit in front of a Three Masted Schooner tied up in front of Tai Pilot.

A majority of the men folk, living in Borth-y-Gest at this time, were associated with boats or the sea in one way or the other.

(postcard by G.A.MorrisRochester)

Taid (grandfather) had run away, like many young boys of the time, to go to sea. He joined the old sailing ships taking slates from Porthmadog all over the world. From South America guano(bird droppings)would be brought back to made into fertilizer.

Taid can be seen, in the middle of the back row, with the crew of the Evelyn. All in this photograph were the sons of master mariners.

Here again, on a postcard by G.H.Morris of Rochester, Taid can be seen on the left, with the crew of the Swanhilda registered in Glasgow. Being a sailor in the old sailing ships was a hazardous occupation. Many families in Porthmadog and Borth-y-Gest knew of someone who had perished at sea.

This postcard, by J.Allan Jones of Criccieth, shows the wreck of the "Owen Morris" at Black Rock Sands, which is not far from Borth-y-Gest.

The Wreck of the "Owen Morris" at Black Rock, Criccieth, December, 1907.
Copyright Photo by J.Allen Jones, Criccieth.

In the 1870's and 80's Porthmadog was a very busy port as this postcard by a local publisher T.A.Morris shows.

PORTMADOC HARBOUR 1878.

During his time at sea Taid was shipwrecked while sailing in the barque " Primera" in the Atlantic Ocean. It caught fire on August 4th 1902, Latitude 28 South, Longitude 13 West. After 25 days adrift in an open boat and 4 days without water, he and nine other of the crew were rescued off Ascension Island. They were taken to a hospital on the Island and nurtured back to health on turtle soup.

Taid, third from the right, sits with the rest of his shipmates, on dry land, in the boat that they were rescued in.

The rescued crew with Taid sitting on the right of the front row.

The hospital on Ascension Island were the crew relaxed and recovered.

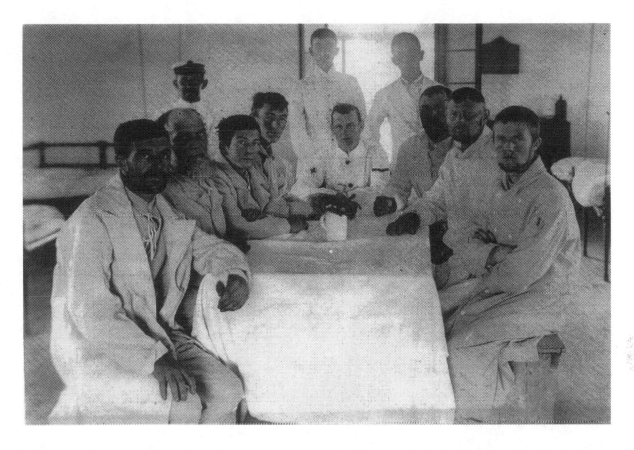

Taid had also lost a leg with his hazardous exploits. An accident had occurred while loading slates at Porthmadog, as depicted in this reproduction postcard by Gwynedd Archives.

The slates were quarried in Blaenau Ffestiniog and were transported to Porthmadog by way of a narrow gauge railway.

Today the trains carry tourists as these two postcards show.

The first is in the Valentine series and the second a Frith card.

On his retirement from the sea, Taid found a job delivering bread with a horse and cart. It was similar to this scene in the Lake District as depicted by this postcard published in the Pettitt's Prize Medal Series Keswick.

The old Post Office in Borth-y-Gest, which published some of the postcards in this book, was also the bakery. At the rear there were large ovens and the local people, who only had a fire to cook with in those days, would take their food along to be cooked in the ovens after the bread had been made.

Taid would take the road out of Porthmadog, as in this postcard by Lilywhite Ltd., with his horse and cart to Morfa Bychan.

In the early 1900's bartering was prevalent. Morfa Bychan had some good fertile soil and Taid would take bread on his rounds and bring back home some fresh vegetables.

Later in life Taid became the car park attendant on the front at Borth-y-Gest.

Taid can be seen, with his white sun hat on, collecting the money, in this postcard published by Harvey Barton.

Two more postcards showing the car park at Borth-y-Gest, the first is in the Frith series the second is published by Valentine.

I recall Taid coming home, at the end of the day, with his fellow attendant, to count the money collected on the car park and to check it tallied with the number of tickets sold.

Little has changed on the front at Borth-y-Gest, although the road and the sea wall has been upgraded. In this old postcard, publisher unknown, the children seem to be enthralled with the photographer and the advent of photography.

In this first postcard, published by R.Griffiths of the old Post Office, the road leading into the village can be seen before the present sea wall was constructed. The second card by Valentine shows the new wall.

This postcard by Frith looks across to Morven, just to the left of the sheds on the front. In the foreground is the Afon Bach(small river).It was here, as a child, just like Winnie the Pooh, I spent hours playing Pooh sticks. It was also a good place to look under stones and catch small eels to put in a bucket.

The view on this Raphael Tuck postcard looks towards the then shops in the village. It's a view I looked out on many days, as it's taken from the front garden of Morven.

When the cows came down to the water on the Traeth, as in this Photochrome postcard, it was said to be a sign of good hot weather. The view is taken from Craig-y-Don.

30819. BORTH-Y-GEST.

Craig-y-Don dominates the front on the Traeth.

These two postcards, the first by R.Griffiths of the Post Office again, show it in all its glory prior to the houses being built on the hill above. The mountains Cnicht and Moelwyn can be seen in the far distance.

CYNICHT & MOELWYN FROM BORTH Y GEST

THE HARBOUR, BORTHYGEST.

In this Photochrome postcard, Craig-y-Don can be seen being built. When I lived in Borth-y-Gest it was the home of Showell Styles who wrote some travel books and was also an accomplished painter.

The following postcards are all taken from Craig-y-Don looking out onto Borth-y-Gest.

This first card by Frith looks towards Borth Farm and the old dairy with Moel-y-Gest in the background.

Moving left and the shops come into view again on this card by Photochrome Co.Ltd.

Left again and Morven and Tai Pilot come into view on this Photochrome card.

This card is published by Valentine and is a later view showing cars on the parking ground.

What better than to sit in the sun and survey the village before you in this postcard by Salmon.

Boats figure prominently on old postcards of Borth-y-Gest. All these cards date back to the early 20th century.

published by Kingsway

published by Wm.Pike 63 High Street Porthmadog.

Published by Photochrome Co.Ltd.

Published by Lloyd & Sons Porthmadog

Not surprisingly messing about in boats was a popular pastime at Borth-y-Gest.

This used card, publisher unknown, was posted in 1908 but dates back much earlier to the late 19th century. Note the building in the background, prior to Craig-y-Don, here was one of the boat building yards.

42719. BORTH-Y-GEST: THE HARBOUR.

Again an old postcard by Photochrome showing Borth Farm and the old buildings on Craig-y-Don's site.

Two more old Postcards ,the first by Frith and the second by Photochrome.

BORTH-Y-GEST Y TRAETH

This postcard is published by R. Griffiths at the local Post Office.

There was great excitement in the village when a BIG boat passed by. The Florence Cook brought in raw material for the explosives factory at Penrhyndeudraeth, deemed a quiet site during the First World War for the Cook's Explosive Factory. Whether any of the materials came from France, but it seemed to also herald the arrival of "Jonnie Onion" who used to come round selling his wares on his bike.

I was introduced to the pleasures of boating at an early age.

Here practising on dry land with my brother,

Later being able to row on the Traeth.

One of the highlights of the summer was the Annual Regatta where sailing, rowing and swimming races took place.

Other highlights included Sportsday. This was held on the Traeth when there were neap tides as shown in this postcard posted in 1934.

Each year I recall watching the runners returning from the seven mile marathon. The runners would come down the hill in the centre of the postcard and the cheering and clapping would begin.

I would spend days prior to the sports day practicing my Roger Bannister thing. Here on the left I take part in the three legged race.

The Traeth would also be the venue for an impromptu game of football for the village youth, as shown in this postcard by Photochrome Co.Ltd.

The annual Carnival was an important occasion for the village. The day would begin with the arrival, on the car park, of white charabancs bringing the Brass Band from Penrhyndeudraeth and a troupe of Morris Dancers. Both would lead the Carnival procession around the village.

In these photographs I take part in the procession as King Farouk at the time of the Suez Crisis in the first one and my brother is the captain of the Florence Cook in the second.

Here I am dressed as Father Time.

My brother ,on the left, as one of the seven dwarfs on a carnival float.

Each year everyone joined in the camera shoot at Garreg Llam.

All around the land November 5th was celebrated. Here I stand in front of the village bonfire on the car park.

All the following postcards look towards The Point, where the trees grow. This is the path to the beach or Garreg Goch. The age of the postcard can be deduced from the height of the trees.

Portmadoc.   Borth y Gest.

This card published by Wrench and printed in Saxony dates back to the beginning of the 20th century .

published by R.Griffiths

published by Valentine & Sons

published by Frith Ltd.

Evening, The Harbour, Borth-y-Gest.

18080

published by J.Salmon Ltd.

Unusual views of Borth-y-Gest taken from the River Glaslyn and looking to the point. From the size of the trees on this postcard, publisher unknown, it dates back to the 19th century. The house behind is Bronafon.

A more recent postcard showing that the trees have grown. This is published by SS Photos Blackpool.

While I have swum in the Traeth when the tide was in, it was quite dangerous to venture into the River Glaslyn with the tide out as in this Photochrome card.
The bathing beaches were round to the left at Garreg Goch.

Again looking from the river in this card by Frith. Just beyond the white boat to the left was the Sedd Fawr(big seat)on Pen Bank.

It was on Sedd Fawr that the "Elders" of the village used to meet to put the world to rights. Here Taid, on the left, sits putting his point of view and surveying the scene.

The following postcards show the view from Pen Bank and Sedd Fawr.

Judges Ltd. Of Hastings

Valentine & Sons

Raphael Tuck & Sons

Valentine & Sons Ltd.

F.Frith Co.Ltd.

Harvey Barton & Sons Ltd.

Judges Ltd.

Valentine & Sons Ltd.

Lillywhite

F.Frith Co. Ltd.

F.Frith Co. Ltd.

F.Frith Co. Ltd.

Leaving Pen Bank is the path to Garreg Goch, the beach, as shown in the next postcards. It is a path I have trod many times, armed with bucket and spade as in the first postcard published by J.Salmon Ltd.In my childhood the days seemed to be permanently hot and sunny. Every day I would look forward to be living in and out of the water and to be making "ice cream factories" in the soft sand at the water's edge. Bits of slate would be used as wafers and then I'd go round selling my wares.

The Point, Borth-y-Gest.   18087.

F.Frith Co.Ltd.

BORTH-Y-GEST.

40198

Harvey Barton & Sons Ltd.

These two cards, the first by Lillywhite Ltd. and the second publisher unknown, show cars which tried to drive to the beach.

CRAIG-Y-DON. BORTH-Y-GEST.

View from Craig-y-Don, Borth-y-Gest.

Eventually, to stop all these cars transgressing, signs had to be erected and these unfortunately hid the fine views.

These two cards show clearly how the area across the Traeth, above Craig-y-Don, has been developed. The older card first is by A.Wells while the second, more modern card ,is by Frith.

Harbour and Cae'r Ogo, Borth-y-gest.

A.WELLS

Looking in the opposite direction to the previous cards, the first glimpse of Garreg Goch comes into view.

Carreg Goch, Borth-y-Gest

41061

Valentine

In this card, by Lloyd & Sons of Porthmadog, the little girls in the foreground, all dressed in their Sunday best, look to have been stage managed to pose for the camera.

Lloyd & Son]   GARREG GOCH.—Borth-y-gest.   [Portmadoc.

These postcards, all published by Photochrome at the beginning of the 20th century, look down on Garreg-Goch Cyntaf (the first beach). Note all the people in the photographs are all dressed in their best clothes, as was the fashion in those days.

42722. Borth-y-gest, Carreg-Goch.

42722 Borth-y-Gest. Carreg-Goch,

The young writer of this next card says he catches the best prawns by the rocks front left.

CARRIG GOCH,
BORTH-Y-GEST.

The publisher of these next three postcards is unknown but they are more than a hundred years old.

In the first, four children pose for the camera. There was little chance of them getting sun burnt. Did their parents know something then?

Even when swimming not too much bare skin could be shown.

BATHING AT CARREG GOCH, BORTH-Y-GEST.

The boat in the background of the previous card, acted as a tug for the bigger boats entering Porthmadog.

The message on the back of this next Photochrome card reads,"The Heart family in the foreground behind pool".

Another early card showing the Victorians in their finery at Garreg Goch. There was no evidence of bathing huts to wheel swimmers into the sea as happened in more fashionable resorts at those times.

These next three cards belong to the 1930's.

This first postcard published by Kingsway shows many people enjoying themselves on the beach.

In this Photochrome postcard, although in the 30's, people are still fully dressed .Note the number of tents. Tents could be hired for the week or for the season.

It was quite safe to leave all your belongings in the tent overnight.

Another Photochrome card shows people relaxing. I recall the man, who hired out the tents, passing Morven every morning, on his bike, going to work.

This postcard by R.Griffiths shows a busy scene with a little boy at the foot of the steps which lead down to the first beach.

BORTH-Y-GEST, GARREG GOCH CLIFFS.

The steps can be seen better in this postcard by Lillywhite and dated 1932. Every year I used to look forward to the C.S.S.M. (Children's Special Service Mission) coming to Borth-y-Gest. They came for two weeks and every morning, on the beach just to the left below the steps, a half hour service would be held singing and praising Jesus.

With other children, I would spend time building a huge sand pulpit. We would then go and collect wild flowers to decorate a text on the front of it. I can still hear the tones of the small pedal organ, wafting across the beach, as we sang to Jesus.

Although this Photochrome postcard shows the beach at Criccieth, it shows a similar service in progress. Everyone was welcome. Afternoons for the children were spent having Teddy Bear Picnics, games on the beach and exciting Treasure Hunts.

An old postcard looking from the first beach towards the second beach and beyond to Garreg-Goch Pella(Far Beach),where the two old sailing ships can be seen. This card was published by R.Griffiths of the Post Office.

Garreg-Goch, Borth-y-gest

Two views looking back to Garreg-Goch Cyntaf, the first by Frith and the second by Valentine. The tents can be seen on the beach.

The path leading to Garreg-Goch Pella as depicted in these next two cards, the first by Valentine. If my mother felt good on the day, we would walk to the far beach, it took a few minutes longer but for me it was the best beach.

CARREG GOCH, BORTH-Y-GEST.   W.4271.

Perhaps the reason I considered Garreg-Goch Pella the best was that it was close to the beach café, known as Café Stokes after the family who ran it.

It was situated close to these two postcards showing the path down to the beach. The first card is published by W.H.S.& S.Ltd.LDN. How good the tray of tea and scones, or ice cream and squash, would taste as you sat on the sand in the sun.

These next two postcards, published by Photochrome from the early 1900s, show that the beach was very popular with lots of tents in evidence.

GARREG GNWC, BORTH-Y-GEST.

BORTH-Y-GEST. GARREG GNWC BAY.

These more modern cards show the beach with all its tents through from the 40's to the 60's

Kingsway

Frith

Publishes by R.Griffiths again, this card shows a building above the tents on the left. This was Borth Fechan Farm which also doubled as a tea shop.

I thought I was really grown up when my mother allowed me to take part in the "Sausage Sizzle" – an early form of bar-b-cue. This took place on a couple of evenings with the CSSM. In the very front foreground of this Salmon postcard is a place, which was known as Garreg Sausage Sizzle, a small outcrop of rock on a path next to Borth Fechan Farm. Here a fire would be lit and sausages cooked on a griddle and hymns sung as the sun set over Garreg-Goch.

The Estuary, Borth-y-Gest.

Garreg Sausage Sizzle was on a path which led to Samson's Bay at Morfa Bychan. The Bay got its name from a huge boulder, known as Samson's rock, which perches precariously above it. It is said that Samson, the strong man of the Bible, lifted the rock into position and his handprints can be seen on the rock to this day!

Samson's rock is in fact a fine example of a perched erratic boulder as this postcard shows. It is made of Snowdonian Acclomorite and deposited during the Ice Age as it passed over Moel-y-Gest.

Garreg Samson, Borth-y-Gest

When spending my six week summer holidays at Borth-y-Gest, I remember that my father could only be with us for two of those weeks because of his work commitment. It was during that time that he would sometimes drive us to Black Rock Sands at Morfa Bychan.

Here you would be able to drive onto the beach. I recall, though, having to help push the car many times at the entrance where sand had been churned up by the many cars as in this Frith postcard.

MFAB.141F. BLACK ROCK SANDS. MORFA BYCHAN.

Once onto the beach there were miles of golden sand with safe bathing, as depicted by these two cards, first by Lillywhite and the second by Valentine.

BLACK ROCK SANDS NEAR TREFLYS

The added attraction of Black Rock was the sea, where great fun could be had diving into the huge waves ,which were a permanent feature of the beach, as shown in this postcard by Frith.

PTMC. 107. BLACK ROCK SANDS. PORTMADOC. Copyright Frith Ltd

Over the years my family have repeated the habits of old and wended their way down to Garreg-Goch to enjoy its delights.

If the weather happened not to favour sitting on the beach, then fishing off the rocks was a good way to pass the day, as in this postcard by Bamforth &Co.Ltd.

This card by Photochrome shows another fisherman on rocks between Borth-y-Gest and Porthmadog.

Looking down the hill to the Traeth, the Post Office was at the bottom on the left. It had been opened as a general stores in 1860 when Borth-y-Gest had become busy with its ship building. The proprietor, a Mr.Lewis Jones, became the first sub-postmaster in 1880.He had come to the village from Liverpool and the stores were first called Liverpool House and the street today is called Mersey Street.

Again looking down on Borth-y-Gest in this postcard by R.Griffiths of the Post Office.The road into the village curves round the Traeth.

These three postcards are from the early 1900's, before houses were built behind Craig-y-Don. The first is published by R.Griffiths, the second by W.A.& S. in the Grovenor Series and the last one by Photochrome.

BORTH-Y-GEST FROM SUNSET HILL

Borth-Y-Gest, Cnicht & Moelwyn. P. 82.

This postcard published by Photo-Precision Ltd. St.Albans shows Cnicht and Moelwyn in the background.

The Cob can be seen in the background of this postcard published by Raphael Tuck &Sons Ltd. The Cob was an embankment, built by William Alexander Maddocks to reclaim acres of land which was regularly flooded by the sea. The Cob was completed in 1811 and aided the development of the new town and deep water harbour of Porthmadog in 1821. A road was also built to link with Port Dinllaen near Nefin, to try and win the race for a route for trade from London to Ireland via a West Coast sea port. This race was eventually lost with a new road being built via Betws-y-Coed and Capel Curig and onto Holyhead.

Here in this Valentine postcard you look across to Talsarnau and, beyond the headland, on the right is Portmeirion, the mock Italian Village built by Clough William Ellis.

The postcard of Portmeirion published by Judges. It was here that the cult television series "The Prisoner" was filmed.

Looking across to the background of this card by Valentine, you can see the granite hill which is still quarried today. The age of a postcard can sometimes be determined by the size and amount of hill still standing.

A postcard here published by Harvey Barton. On the land in the left foreground an estate of new modern houses has been built today.

With the advent of aerial photography, more adventurous views were added to postcards. This card below is published by Raphael Tuck.

Both of these next two cards, first by R.Griffiths, look out onto the bay, where just to the right, The River Glaslyn meets the River Dwyryd flowing in from Maentwrog.

The second one shows the wide and dangerous expanse of the Glaslyn Estuary. Borth-y-Gest was ,in the past, the starting point for one of the major crossings of this area. The locals would earn precious farthings guiding strangers across the treacherous sands of Traeth Mawr, at low tide, to Harlech on the other side.
The source of the income disappeared when William Maddocks opened the Cobb in 1811.

As shown in this Frith postcard, the road out of Porthmadog to Borth-y-Gest is uphill to start with, until the crest of the hill is reached.

The next cards show the houses on the road leading to Borth-y-Gest after descending down the hill.

A Frith postcard taken from Borth Woods.

A card by R.Griffiths. The Cob can be clearly seen.

A Photochrome card, the granite hill in the background was quite big then .

A closer look at the road into Borth-y-Gest coming down through the trees. This card is by Lloyd & Sons of Porthmadog.

Two ladies chat on the road further into the village.

This postcard, by Raphael Tuck, is taken on the road from Garreg Goch back into the village, Pen Bank is on the right. The empty street suggests it was taken before the advent of tourism. The bed and breakfast trade thrived through the 50's and 60's and into the 70's.

In case you couldn't choose which was the best view for your postcard home, the publishers introduced multi-view cards.

Photochrome

Salmon

Photo Precision

Salmon

Valentine

Modern Postcards today still depict people messing around in boats and in colour, can show Borth in all its glory.

J. Arthur Dixon

Salmon

John Jones Ruthin

Borth-y-Gest

John Jones Ruthin

Tourists still visit Borth-y-Gest today many as day trippers, some staying B&B and some renting holiday houses.. The tents for hire have gone from Garreg Goch and the summers no longer seem to be as hot. Many of the houses in the village are now holiday homes.

Children now leave the village to seek employment elsewhere ending up all over the world not unlike the sailors of old.   More people may get to know about Borth as the Welsh Television S4C has filmed a series of children's programmes based in Borth-y-Gest called Cei Bach which show lovely glimpses of the village and should ensure visitors come and see the magnificent scenery.

Time moves on but as this Valentine postcard says
"Hooray for a Holiday in Borth-y-Gest"

Hooray! for a
Holiday at BORTH-Y-GEST

My mother died on Boxing Day 2002 and is buried in a family grave alongside the small chapel at Treflys, as shown in this Fine Arts postcard by Christian Novels Publishing Co. Treflys lies on a hill between Borth-y-Gest and Criccieth, at the foot of Moel-y-Gest and overlooking Cardigan Bay.

Treflys Church, Criccieth.

Cysgwch Mam Cysgwch
Rest in Peace

About the Author

I am a retired school teacher having taught in four different Junior schools spanning forty years.I was born at the hospital in Bangor North Wales and lived the first six years of my life in my mothers home village of Borth-y-Gest near Portmadoc in Caernarvonshire.My father was in the army having met my mother in a holiday romance on one of his leaves from the army.

When the war was over he took us to live in his home village(as it was then)of Maghull,which is seven miles North of Liverpool where at first we lived in a Prefab.Every holiday was spent back in Borth-y-Gest.

The war had left my father an ill man and he died at the early age of fifty-one.My father was English speaking and my mother Welsh.Having seemed to have spent most of my life with my mother, who died only recently, I speak fluent Welsh.

Holidays in Borth-y-Gest continued for me into my college days and today my brother has bought a holiday apartment nearby and his children and grandchildren spend many holidays there.